Romans 13-16
and Galatians

Romans 13-16 and Galatians

KENNETH O. GANGEL

VICTOR BOOKS ®

A DIVISION OF SCRIPTURE PRESS PUBLICATIONS INC.
USA CANADA ENGLAND

Recommended Dewey Decimal Classification: 227
Suggested Subject Heading: BIBLE, N.T.–EPISTLES

Library of Congress Catalog Card Number: 89-60166
ISBN: 0-89693-729-1

VICTOR BOOKS
A division of SP Publications, Inc.
Wheaton, Illinois 60187

CONTENTS

How to Use This Study

Personal Growth Bible Studies are designed to help you understand God's Word and how it applies to everyday life. To complete the studies in this book, you will need to use a Bible. A good modern translation of the Bible, such as the *New International Version* or the *New American Standard Bible*, will give you the most help. (NOTE: the questions in this book are based on the *New International Version.*)

You will find it helpful to follow a similar sequence with each study. First, read the introductory paragraphs. This material helps set the tone and lay the groundwork for the passage to be studied. Once you have completed this part of the study, spend time reading the assigned passage in your Bible. This will give you a general feel for the contents of the passage.

Having completed the preliminaries, you are then ready to dig deeper into the Scripture passage. Each study is divided into several sections so that you can take a close-up look at the smaller parts of the larger passage. These sections each begin with a synopsis of the Scripture to be studied in that section. Following each synopsis is a two-part study section made up of *Explaining the Text* and *Examining the Text*.

Explaining the Text gives background notes and commentary to help you understand points in the text that may not be readily apparent. After reading any comments that appear in *Explaining the Text*, answer each question under *Examining the Text*.

At the end of each study is a section called *Experiencing the Text*. The questions in this section focus on the application of biblical principles to life. You may find that some of the questions can be answered immediately; others will require that you spend more time reflecting on the passages you have just studied.

The distinctive format of the Personal Growth Bible Studies makes them easy to use individually as well as for group study. If the majority of those in your group answer the questions before the group meeting, spend most of your time together discussing the *Experiencing* questions.

If, on the other hand, members have not answered the questions ahead of time and you have adequate time in your group meeting, work through all of the questions together.

However you use this series of studies, our prayer is that you will understand the Bible as never before, and that because of this understanding, you will experience a rich and dynamic Christian life. If questions of interpretation arise in the course of this study, we recommend you refer to the two-volume set, *The Bible Knowledge Commentary*, edited by John F. Walvoord and Roy B. Zuck (Victor Books, 1984, 1986).

Introduction to the Epistles to the Romans and the Galatians

These are days in which questions about the nature of the Gospel have been elevated to the level of controversy. Theologians argue about how one comes to faith and what it means to repent. Emotional phrases like "lordship salvation" and "cheap grace" are bantered about in popular magazines and heard commonly on religious radio and television. This would obviously be a good time to get back to the Bible on these crucial issues.

No better source can be found for our understanding of the doctrine of justification by faith than a combination of Romans and Galatians. These books are so closely intertwined that some colleges and seminaries actually teach them as one course. Donald Campbell notes that Romans "has been considered by some to be an expansion of Galatians and [Galatians] has been called 'a short Romans'" (*The Bible Knowledge Commentary*, Victor).

The break in our study comes at a logical point as Paul segues in Romans 12 from a strong doctrinal section to the application of doctrine. Chapters 13–16 are intensely practical, focusing on how God's righteousness can be revealed in the transformed lives of His people.

Since we "introduced" the Book of Romans in the study of chapters 1–12, perhaps we can focus here on Galatians. But the natural unity of the books must occupy our minds throughout the study. Someone has suggested that the Epistle to the Galatians relates to the Book of Romans as does a rough model to a finished statue. Along with the emphasis on justification by faith, Paul uses both epistles to emphasize life in the Spirit, the possession of newborn children of God. This close affinity, however, does not allow us to make the larger and more familiar book a standard for interpreting the shorter epistle. We must analyze and understand Galatians in itself. Remember the letters were sent to two different places in the ancient world.

There is very little argument about the authorship of Galatians and the purpose also seems clear—to affirm the Gospel and vindicate Paul's apostleship in the light of false teaching and attacks by the Judaizers. Galatia was a Roman province in Asia Minor (Turkey), and most evangelical scholars agree that the letter was addressed primarily to the churches of South Galatia, which would include Derbe, Lystra, Iconium, and Pisidian Antioch.

One important theme of the book certainly centers on Christian *freedom*, a word which appears in some form 11 times in the book. Paul insists that salvation by faith in Jesus alone is all that one requires for salvation. Believers are not obligated to keep the law either to obtain or retain salvation. Other key words include *Gentiles* (10 times), *grace* (7 times), *circumcision* (13 times), and *faith* (26 times).

Small wonder Galatians was popular right from the start. In the second century Irenaeus quotes 25 verses from the book and after A.D. 200 it is commonly discussed in literature of both the Eastern and Western churches. In modern times Galatians, like Romans, came into prominence largely through the influence of Martin Luther in the Protestant Reformation. Today this practical treatment of doctrine and lifestyle remains as relevant as if Paul wrote to all the evangelical churches in the Western hemisphere this very year.

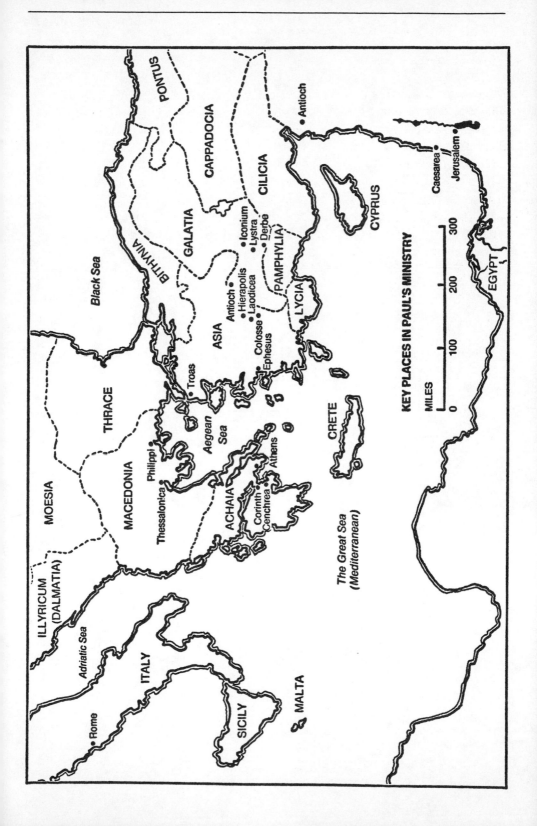

KEY PLACES IN PAUL'S MINISTRY

MILES

0   100   200   300

Romans 13:1-14

Christian Relationships

During the 1980s Americans observed constant conflict between a President from one political party and a Congress largely dominated by the other party. Charges of the "imperial presidency" or "imperial Congress" were hurled back and forth on Capitol Hill. Meanwhile, many questioned whether two terms of a conservative presidency genuinely strengthened the evangelical church.

One thing seems clear as we open Romans 13—the people of God must not look to secular government to advance the cause of the Gospel; whether it does or not, they are to be in subjection to properly appointed governmental authority. Chapter 13 moves us from the Christian's duty in the church (chapter 12) to the Christian's duty toward the state. Interestingly, this was a hot topic among first-century Christians just as it is in our day. You remember Jesus had announced that His kingdom was not of this world and had called His disciples to be in the world but not of the world (John 17:15-18). Now in the middle of the first century, Christians wondered what that meant in actual life, and Paul feels constrained to devote an entire section of his letter to the issue, quite properly addressed to believers living at the seat of government in Rome.

One possible key word of the passage is *relationship*. Dealing with the believer's relationship to government, law, and the Lord, the apostle demonstrates how these intertwine since one's commitment to the Lord will determine how he or she responds to both law and authority.

In this chapter, Paul reminds his readers that all duly constituted government functions by divine sanction and, therefore, only evildoers need fear it. For Christians, obedience comes not from terror but from conscience—the recognition that citizenship in heaven only improves and enhances citizenship on earth.

A. RELATIONSHIP TO THE GOVERNMENT (*Rom. 13:1-7*). Paul begins this section by dealing with the authority of the state, and his observation is distinctly Christian—no authority exists except that which God has established. Almost 2,000 years later we wonder about the accuracy of such a statement, until we remember that God's sovereign control of His universe has been a timeless principle confirmed by the psalmist (Ps. 75:6-7), by Daniel (Dan. 4:25, 32), and by the Lord Jesus Himself (John 19:10-11). Government has a distinct responsibility to promote good and punish evil, and Christians have a distinct obligation to obey governmental authority.

Examining the Text	*Explaining the Text*
1. Read Romans 13:1-7. What word appears seven times in the first six verses?	1. Perhaps, rather than arguing for or against capital punishment in itself, these verses more likely support the government's right to use capital punishment if it is deemed necessary.
2. According to this passage, where does governmental authority originate?	
3. What word does Paul use three times to describe government rulers?	
4. For what two reasons were Paul's readers told to submit to authority?	4. The *submission* of which Paul speaks appears as a verb form in the present tense, indicating a habit or lifestyle for believers.
5. How do you understand the difference between taxes and revenue?	

Explaining the Text

Examining the Text

6. How do you think a first-century slave would have responded to this letter?

7. Capture the central theme of these verses in one sentence of ten words or less.

8. The word *wrongdoer* in verse 4 refers to the repeated practice of sinful behavior, not just an occasional slip into error.

8. How can one be released from fear of authority?

9. How do you think Russian Christians might respond to these verses today?

10. Why *do* citizens pay taxes?

B. RELATIONSHIP TO THE LAW (*Rom. 13:8-10*). In this brief section, Paul sounds very much like the Lord Jesus as he emphasizes the dominance of love over the law. Just submitting to the authority of the state does not handle all relationship obligations for the Christian. The positive and active side of Christian living means loving other people, an attitude which enables us to fulfill the perfect law of God.

Explaining the Text

Examining the Text

1. The "no debt" expression of verse 8 is a strongly emphatic construction based on a repetition in the Greek text and is perhaps best translated, "owe nothing to anyone."

1. Read Romans 13:8-10. In conjunction with this study, review Exodus 20:13-17; Deuteronomy 5:17-21; and Leviticus 19:18. What word would you select as the key to these verses?

Examining the Text	*Explaining the Text*
2. Why is the debt to love one another called a "continuing debt"? (v. 8)	2. The word *debt* in verse 8 and the word *owe* in verse 7 come from the same Greek root.
3. Verse 9 contains four out of the five "second table" commandments. Which one is missing? (Explain the terms "second table.")	3. Literally the word for "rule" in verse 9 is *logos*. It is commonly interpreted "word." In the Old Testament, the Ten Commandments are sometimes called the "Ten Words" (Ex. 34:28).
4. What relationship do you see between verses 8-10 and verses 1-7?	
5. In what way does love fulfill the law?	
6. Why would Paul, who knew the Old Testament well, say, "Whatever other commandment there may be"? (v. 9)	

C. RELATIONSHIP TO THE LORD (*Rom. 13:11-14*). As the light draws closer, the night becomes more intense. As Christians sense the coming of the Lord drawing near, they have even greater responsibility to "put on the armor of light" and behave like people in whom the living Christ dwells.

Examining the Text	*Explaining the Text*
1. Read Romans 13:11-14. How do you suppose the Roman Christians had been "slumbering"?	

Explaining the Text	*Examining the Text*
	2. At least five times Paul uses a time reference in these verses. Can you find them?
	3. To what might Paul have been referring by "the day"?
4. The word *decently* in verse 13 once meant what the word *honorable* means today—attractive and dependable.	4. List six things we are *not* to do, according to verse 13.
5. Verse 13 suggests that one sin leads to another, and together they lead to blaming other people for our problems.	5. Select substitute words (synonyms) for the six things you identified in question 4.
6. The secret to living chaste lives in a time of darkness is a close relationship with the Lord Jesus Christ (Eph. 4:24; Col. 3:10; Gal. 3:27).	6. Describe what you think Paul meant by "clothe yourself with the Lord Jesus Christ."
7. The latter part of verse 14 is a strong negation—"stop thinking about how to gratify the desire of the sinful nature."	7. What is a "sinful nature"?
	8. Why does the NIV use "sinful nature" in the text and "flesh" in the margin?

Experiencing the Text

1. What implications (if any) does verse 7 hold for the common practice of buying on credit?

2. In what ways should Christians be the best citizens of any society?

3. Name some ways people violate verses 1-7 today.

4. What specific officers in today's society might parallel the "governing authorities" of verse 1?

5. Name 10 people to whom you owe an outstanding debt of love.

6. Suggest at least three ways you pay the love debt to family members.

7. Verse 9 says "love your neighbor as yourself." How do you love yourself?

8. How do Christians get themselves into spiritual trouble by "thinking about how to gratify the desires of the sinful nature"?

9. Name several ways you can "clothe" your children or friends with the Lord Jesus Christ.

10. Write a newspaper headline heralding the message of this chapter.

Romans 14

Accepting the Weak

How many questions of modern Christians are covered by the principles of this chapter! For years Christians have argued about the use of alcohol and tobacco, attendance at movies and plays, participating in certain activities on Sunday, and a host of other controversial issues. The Bible contains no specific information about most of them, but it does contain general principles about behavioral tolerance, personal convictions, suspended judgment, and mutual edification.

This chapter speaks clearly about balance in the Christian life. On the one hand, we need to welcome and tolerate the views of others even though they may seem strange to us. On the other hand, we must keep our own habits above criticism, recognizing that the citizens of God's kingdom are marked by righteousness and joy, not by rituals and practices.

The end goal of all of this is the building up of believers and the strengthening of the body. People in almost any congregation come in different sizes, shapes, and levels of spiritual maturity. These varying degrees of biblical discernment create differences of opinion and can lead to church fights and splits. This chapter parallels 1 Corinthians 8–10 and together they offer practical guidelines for applying the principles of heaven while living on earth. Let's remember too that the weak brother is not necessarily less moral or more questionable in his behavior. In fact, he's more likely to be scrupulously pious but impaired by a limited understanding of Christian truth and freedom. The behavior of the "strong Christian" may actually be more questionable than that of the "weak Christian," so Paul calls those more mature and, therefore, more responsible to bring their lives into line with the needs of others in the church.

A. BEHAVIORAL TOLERANCE (*Rom. 14:1-4*). Diet was a real problem to many early converts, especially Jews. What about things offered to idols? What about flesh instead of herbs? The main thing is to recognize that judgment for these "peculiarities" does not belong to us as fellow Christians.

Explaining the Text

1. The word translated "accept" in verse 1 conveys the sense of warmheartedness (Acts 18:26; 28:2).

2. The words *disputable matters* refer to quarrels about opinions. These things believers are not to engage in.

3. The words *look down on* in verse 3 are also found in Romans 14:10 and could also be translated "despise" or "reject with contempt."

Examining the Text

1. Read Romans 14:1-4. Paul is famous for rhetorical questions. Pick out the one in this section.

2. What connection do you see between the beginning of chapter 14 and the end of chapter 13?

3. Choose one or more of the following options to complete this sentence: These four verses attack the sin of _____ in Christians.
   a. complaining
   b. pride
   c. criticism
   d. envy

4. Who is this "servant" of verse 4?

5. Why will the servant surely "stand"?

6. How do you see a difference between the weaker brother and the legalist or Judaizer?

B. PERSONAL CONVICTIONS (*Rom. 14:5-8*). Christian beliefs and behavior must not be put on like a borrowed coat and returned when no longer needed. Each person should determine his or her own convictions and carry them out as unto the Lord. In short, the apostle tells everybody to mind his or her own business, or at least focus on a vertical comparison (with the Lord) rather than a horizontal (with other people).

Examining the Text	*Explaining the Text*
1. Read Romans 14:5-8. Who among the recipients of this letter would have been most likely to fuss about special days?	1. Like the submission to the government of 13:1, the convictions of 14:5 represent a lifestyle and a long-term commitment.
2. What special days would the early believers have argued about?	
3. A key three-word prepositional phrase appears six times in these verses. Find it and write it.	
4. What attitude should characterize both "meat eaters" and "abstainers"?	4. At stake throughout this section, and indeed the entire chapter, is the believer's individual accountability to the Lord in all areas of his or her life and doctrine.
5. What connection does living and dying have with keeping special days and eating or not eating meat?	5. Notice that death does not end the struggle but is to be viewed as an enlarged opportunity to glorify God.

C. SUSPENDED JUDGMENT (*Rom. 14:9-18*). All Christians are equally servants of the Lord, and He alone stands as their judge. Since we all will have to give an account of our behavior to God, we should never place stumbling blocks in another believer's way. The ultimate goal of godly living is a good reputation and unity in the body, rather than the exercise of individual rights.

Explaining the Text	*Examining the Text*
	1. Read Romans 14:9-18. According to these verses, why did Christ die and return to life?
	2. How is Christ the Lord of the dead?
3. God's judgment seat in verse 10 is probably to be identified with the Judgment Seat of Christ (2 Cor. 5:10).	3. Name at least two reasons why it is wrong to judge other Christians.
4. A stumbling block (*proskoma*) is something against which someone may strike his foot. But an obstacle (*skandalon*) depicts a trap designed to catch a victim.	4. What kinds of stumbling blocks do Christians today put in each other's way?
	5. What do you think verse 14 means?
6. The word *righteousness* in verse 17 refers not to justification or salvation but rather to proper behavior.	6. Name the three characteristic ingredients of God's kingdom.
	7. How can Christians "destroy" their brothers and sisters?

D. MUTUAL EDIFICATION (*Rom. 14:19-23*). If any question exists about a certain behavior of Christians, Paul offers an important principle—don't do it. As important as freedom becomes for the believer, a righteous lifestyle which offers no offense nor cause of stumbling to others takes the priority.

Examining the Text

Explaining the Text

1. Read Romans 14:19-23. What food(s) might some of Paul's readers have thought unclean?

1. The word *clean* in verse 20 means free from impurities, not mixed with unwanted elements.

2. In what ways can believers engage in mutual edification?

2. As we compare this passage with 1 Corinthians 8, we understand that Paul commends to the Roman Christians what had already become a lifestyle for himself.

3. For what valid reasons should one *not* "eat" or "drink"?

3. In verse 21 eating and drinking are not lifestyle patterns but individual acts. In other words, don't do anything even once if it will cause your brother to stumble.

4. How does verse 22 compare with the usual idea of standing up for convictions?

5. To what might the word *doubts* refer in verse 23?

5. The word *faith* in verse 23 appears the same way it is used at the beginning of the chapter, the confidence that we are free to do what God wants, not a reference to saving faith.

6. Pick one verse in this section to summarize the chapter.

Experiencing the Text

1. Substitute a few contemporary words for "eat everything" and "only vegetables."

2. Write a six- or seven-word commandment summarizing verses 1-4. For example, "Thou shalt not _____ _____ _____ _____."

3. State some practical ways Christians "live to the Lord" (v. 8).

4. Now state some practical ways Christians "die to the Lord."

5. This chapter must obviously be applied to modern controversial behavior among Christians. Can you name four or five such questionable issues?

6. Name several ways you and I can cause brothers to fall.

7. List some things we should keep just between ourselves and God.

8. Rewrite verse 22 in your own words.

Romans 15

We Who Are Strong

Several years ago one of the elders at my church drove into the parking lot of an apartment complex to give an older lady a ride to a church meeting. It was dark as he stepped out of his car. Out of the darkness, a little five-year-old boy walked up to him and said simply, "Walk with me; I'm scared." The youngster led Bill around the complex until he found his apartment building.

It was a simple helping act but so symbolic—from the darkness to the light; from frightening strangeness to familiarity; from fear to faith; from loneliness to companionship—the precise journey the world needs to make today. That elder assumed the role Paul calls for in our chapter as he addresses those "who are strong."

The argument of the epistle now draws to a close and Paul zeros in on the bull's-eye of his practical target, the demonstration of Jesus Christ in the lives of His followers. In verses 8, 16, 25, 27, and 31 some form of the word *ministry* or *service* appears, and the entire chapter seems to radiate this idea. The first part of the chapter deals with the ministry of Christ and the latter part (almost two thirds) with the ministry of Paul. The apostle wastes no time in getting to the point of following the example of the Lord. When Christians patiently put up with the struggles of those "whose faith is weak" and deliberately go out of their own way to help others, they follow the example of Christ.

The Lord's ministry to Jews is aimed at establishing God's truth and affirming the promises made in the Old Testament era. For the Gentiles, the message focuses on the mercy of God and how awareness of that mercy leads us to glorify Him. Paul himself exemplified God's grace. God had allowed him to obtain sterling qualifications to be a servant of Jesus Christ to the Gentiles, and Paul does not hesitate to remind his readers that God used him and the missionary team widely "from Jerusalem all the way around to Illyricum" (15:19).

A. COMPELLED BY GOD'S GRACE (*Rom. 15:1-13*). Paul continues his argument of the preceding chapter but addresses it specifically to "strong Christians." He encourages the believers by calling upon God to grant them "endurance and encouragement" and "a spirit of unity among yourselves." Those three qualities can adorn any Christian and any church in any age.

Examining the Text	*Explaining the Text*
1. Read Romans 15:1-13. From what we learned in chapter 14, who are the "strong" and who are the "weak"? (v. 1)	
2. According to this passage, where does hope come from? (v. 5)	
3. What is the practical and public result of unity? (v. 6)	
4. For what reason(s) did Christ come?	4. To "accept one another" (v. 7) means to welcome with readiness of spirit, since Christians have equal rights to interpretations and behaviors of conscience.
5. At least five Old Testament passages are quoted in these verses, can you list them by reference?	5. The central thrust of verses 8-12 demonstrates that Christ has fulfilled all the expectations of the Old Testament.
6. Name several things we receive as a result of trusting God (v. 13).	6. Paul's reference to "the God of hope" (v. 13) is intended to remind the readers that only God can inspire true hope and grant it to His children.

B. COMMITTED TO GOD'S CALL (*Rom. 15:14-22*). Paul's ministry was specific and powerful. Nothing seemed more important to him than the fulfilling of the will of God, particularly in the salvation of the Gentiles. By the time he wrote these words, he had traveled through Palestine, Asia Minor, and almost the entire peninsula of Greece. In the process, he had developed a foundational principle for his own work—to preach the Gospel where Christ was not known.

Explaining the Text	*Examining the Text*
1. The word for "instruct" in verse 14 is *noutheteó*, emphasizing the inculcation of truth. In Colossians 3:16 it is translated "counsel," and in 1 Thessalonians 5:14, "warn."	1. Read Romans 15:14-22. How does Paul describe the Roman Christians? (v. 14)
	2. How is proclaiming the Gospel to the Gentiles a "priestly duty"? (v. 16)
	3. What was the result of that proclamation? (v. 16)
4. When Paul says he had been hindered from coming to see the believers at Rome (v. 22), the grammar of the verb suggests that this had happened repeatedly.	4. Find a Bible atlas and locate Illyricum.
	5. How does a quotation from Isaiah 52:15 fit Paul's point in verse 21?

C. CONTROLLED BY GOD'S PLAN (*Rom. 15:23-29*). Paul's work among Gentiles in the east was finished, and he thought perhaps the Spirit would now let him go west to Rome. Of course, he had no idea that he would go not as a missionary but as a prisoner of the state. We learn in Philippians 1:12-20 that Paul's ministry brought great blessing and encouragement to the Roman believers.

Examining the Text	Explaining the Text
1. Read Romans 15:23-29. Find Macedonia and Achaia on a Bible atlas. In what country are they located?	1. The word for "contribution" in verse 26 is the familiar *koinónia* emphasizing the participation and sharing among the believers.
2. In what ways might the Romans "assist" Paul on his journey to Spain? (v. 24)	
3. From what you know about church history, did Paul ever visit Spain?	3. Spain marked the edge of the frontier in the Roman Empire and its obvious needs brought excitement and inspiration to the heart of this pioneer missionary.
4. What is the "fruit" of verse 28?	4. Notice that the contribution to the fellow believers can be viewed both as a gift and an obligation (v. 27).
5. How does one Christian visit another "in the full measure of the blessing of Christ"? (v. 29)	

D. COMFORTED BY GOD'S PEOPLE (*Rom. 15:30-33*). The call goes up for prayer warriors, fellow strugglers to stand by the spiritual side of the pioneer missionary; no broad generalizations here, no "bless the missionaries" praying. The apostle knows precisely what his Roman friends should ask of God.

Examining the Text	Explaining the Text
1. Read Romans 15:30-33. What two motivators does Paul employ to solicit the prayers of Roman believers? (v. 30)	1. The word *rescued* does not emphasize so much removal from danger to safety as it does deliverance from hostility by some dramatic power.

Explaining the Text	*Examining the Text*
2. The grammar of verse 31 suggests that the emphatic word is *acceptable*. Paul spent his whole ministry trying to appease the traditionalists at Jerusalem without compromising the purity of God's grace to the Gentiles.	2. What two requests does he put before them? (v. 31)
	3. What was the "struggle" to which Paul refers? (v. 30)
	4. What fruit of the Spirit did Paul hope to display upon his arrival in Rome? (v. 32)
	5. Verse 33 would seem more appropriate at the end of the letter. Why would it appear here?

Experiencing the Text

1. Suggest several ways "strong" Christians can "bear with the failings of the weak" (v. 1).

2. How can we "please" our neighbors in order to build them up? (v. 2)

3. Memorize Romans 15:4. Type or print it on a 3 x 5 card and put it where you can see it frequently.

4. We commonly talk about overflowing with joy, but name some ways we can "overflow with hope" (v. 13).

5. Verse 14 offers quite a compliment to the readers. Think of several people you know who fit this description. Now thank God for them.

6. Paul uses the phrase "what Christ has accomplished through me." List some things Christ has accomplished through you (v. 18).

7. Think of someone you plan to visit within the next year. How can you design that visit so that you both will be "refreshed?" (v. 32)

8. Think of leaders in your church (pastors, elders, deacons, Sunday School teachers) who need your prayer so that their ministries "will be acceptable to the saints." Write their names somewhere and pray for them throughout the next several weeks.

Romans 16

Greetings and Glory

On Thursday, October 20, 1988, the fifth and final game of the 1988 World Series was played in Oakland, California. Cy Young Award winner Orel Hershiser took the mound for the Dodgers holding a record of 59 scoreless innings during the season and 21⅓ scoreless innings in postseason play.

As he struggled during the first four innings, television camera close-ups showed him in the dugout, head back and eyes closed. During a post-game interview, Bob Costas of NBC Sports asked whether in those moments he was resting, meditating, or thinking about the next inning. "No," said Hershiser, "I was singing hymns to myself."

The sequel to the Costas interview came the next night on "The Tonight Show." When asked by Johnny Carson if he would sing one of those hymns, Hershiser surprised host, studio audience, and millions of viewers with a full rendition of the Doxology!

The many people named in Romans 16 were like Orel Hershiser in one very important way. No, they were not professional athletes. None of them held any sports records that we know about. But they were all willing to give public testimony of their faith in Christ. Though the apostle had never been to Rome at the time he wrote these words, the record of people he knew and had heard of was established among believers around the Mediterranean world.

Actually this chapter tells us about the founding of the church in Rome. It may well have been started by people with whom Paul had contact during his travels; people like Priscilla and Aquila who had worked with the apostle in other places and now lived in Rome. Note too the mixed group of Jews and Gentiles one would expect in the capital city of a pagan government.

Many Bible readers are surprised that Paul knew so many people in Rome, but we dare not forget how easy that ancient government had made communication and travel in the first century. Others express concern that almost all the names are Gentile rather than Jewish. This can be accounted for by recognizing that, like Paul, many citizens either had both Jewish and Gentile names or took Gentile names when living in a distinctive culture like Rome.

Why would Paul name so many people in the letter to the Romans while scarcely mentioning anyone in most of his other epistles? Most commentators suggest it was because he had never been to Rome and, therefore, could not be accused of any favoritism in offering a list of names. To do the same thing with Corinth, for example, might expose him to some nasty criticism.

Whatever your attitude toward the long list of greetings, you must be moved by the closing paragraph and especially the closing sentence, so appropriate to this brilliant Christian letter—"To the only wise God be glory forever through Jesus Christ! Amen" (Rom. 16:27).

A. CHRISTIAN FRIENDS (*Rom. 16:1-16*). Many Bible scholars have concluded that Phoebe may be mentioned at greatest length because she carried this letter to Rome. Then the apostle begins to call the roll of the saints, many of whom are probably his converts. In many cases he links them with some happy experience recalled from shared ministry in times past.

Examining the Text	*Explaining the Text*
1. Read Romans 16:1-16. Locate Cenchrea in a Bible atlas.	
2. How does one receive people "in a way worthy of the saints"? (v. 2)	2. The name *Phoebe* means "bright" or "radiant." Some suggest she was a church officer (deaconess) at Cenchrea, but the word "servant" seems to imply general ministry.
3. Review Luke's words about Priscilla and Aquila in Acts 18:1-4, 18-26.	3. Priscilla and Aquila are never mentioned apart in Scripture; they present a beautiful picture of bonded life and ministry.

Explaining the Text	Examining the Text
4. Tryphena and Trypho- sa may have been sisters since their names sound so much alike. The names mean "dainty" and "deli- cate." Paul speaks of Apel- les (v. 10) as one who was "tested and approved in Christ," a goal Paul had set for himself (1 Cor. 9:27) and for Timothy (2 Tim. 2:15).	4. Paul commends four people who "worked hard." Can you find them? What do they have in common?
	5. If "apostles" refers to only the eleven and Paul, why would this letter include Andronicus and Junias? (v. 7)

B. FALSE TEACHERS (*Rom. 16:17-20*). Even in a spirit of greeting Paul remembers the importance of sound doctrine. As always, false doctrine is most successfully perpetrated by tricky characters with clever words.

Explaining the Text	Examining the Text
	1. Read Romans 16:17-20. How were the Roman be- lievers to handle divisive people? (v. 17)
2. The word *deceive* in verse 18 means "to trick, cheat, or beguile." The emphasis is on the means rather than the result.	2. What kind of people seem most vulnerable to false teaching? (v. 18)
	3. What caused Paul to be "full of joy" over the Romans? (v. 19)

Examining the Text	Explaining the Text
4. Name some ways Christians can be "wise about what is good."	4. The words for "good" and "evil" in verse 19 represent an antithesis; they both focus on the inward quality of the moral or immoral nature.
5. Name some ways Christians can be "innocent about what is evil."	
6. How do you interpret the first phrase of verse 20?	6. The word *crush* in verse 20 may indicate that Paul has in mind the promise of Genesis 3:15.

C. SPECIAL MESSAGES (*Rom. 16:21-24*). How commonly we include brief greetings from family members and friends when writing to someone far away. As word spread that Paul was sending a major letter to Rome, those around him wanted their messages sent along also.

Examining the Text	Explaining the Text
1. Read Romans 16:21-24. What exactly do you think Tertius did with this epistle?	1. Tertius is a Latin name meaning "third."
2. Why was Gaius special to Paul? (See 1 Corinthians 1:14.)	
3. Using a commentary or Bible encyclopedia, identify the city from which Paul wrote Romans.	
4. What might a "director of public works" have done in the first century? Compare other versions (v. 23).	4. It's possible that the Erastus of our passage is the same one referred to in Acts 19:22.

D. ETERNAL GLORY (*Rom. 16:25-27*). Many of the benedictions which we use in modern worship services have come from Paul's letters. Here we find one of the most magnificent of all, verses worth reading, memorizing, and quoting over and over again.

Explaining the Text	*Examining the Text*
1. This is the only time the word *proclamation* appears in the Book of Romans, though it is a common New Testament word (v. 25).	1. Read Romans 16:25-27. What two things could establish the Roman Christians? (v. 25)
	2. What is "the mystery hidden for long ages past"? (vv. 25-26)
3. Some commentators believe the phrase "the command of the eternal God" refers to the great commission given by the Lord to His followers before the Ascension. The NIV omits verse 24 because many of the better manuscripts do not contain it.	3. How was this mystery revealed?
	4. What did God intend to happen as a result of this revelation?
	5. Through what channel does glory get to God?

Experiencing the Text

1. Can you think of any people who might need help from you the way Phoebe did from her Christian friends? (v. 2)

2. Paul thanks God for Christian relatives. How about you?

3. What do you think would be the contemporary counterpart of "a holy kiss"? (v. 16)

4. Name some specific things you do to avoid false teaching. Now add one or two more you might want to do.

5. Think of some people who could profit from your greetings in a letter or a phone call. Why not contact them this week in the spirit of Romans 16?

6. In what ways might you increase or improve your ministry of hospitality? (v. 23)

7. Memorize Romans 16:27.

8. What role can you play in God's plan that all nations might believe and obey Him?

Galatians 1

No Other Gospel

The people living around Lake Geneva in Wisconsin are pressed by law, I am told, "to maintain a footpath" all around that large lake. Yet as one walks around the lake he finds that path made of grass, gravel, sand, old boards, fancy boardwalks with handrails, narrow trails through the trees, and just about any other possible construction. It appears to the casual observer that the property owners have no unified interpretation of what it means to "maintain a footpath."

Paul attacks just such a definitional problem in the Book of Galatians. What precisely is the Gospel? When one uses the term *Gospel*, does it mean one thing for Jews and another for Gentiles? Are there two Gospels or maybe three, each applied selectively to different groups of people considering Christianity in the first century?

Like the latter chapters of the Book of Romans, the Book of Galatians emphasizes grace and freedom. Any time Paul deals with the Gospel he immediately gravitates to the reality of God's grace which liberates us from the law, the rigidity of rules, and the requirements of tradition and ritual.

But who is this apostle so boldly declaring a Gospel of freedom through God's grace? Authority of office, certainty of God's call, and confidence in his message all become sustaining themes throughout this epistle. This first part of the epistle becomes personal as the apostle moves directly from his salutation (complete with credentials) to a rebuke of the Galatians and an affirmation of the authority of the Gospel. He chooses to establish his authority as God's messenger by reviewing the history of his spiritual life. He had been a zealous Jew in Jerusalem, taught by Gamaliel himself. After the death of Stephen and persecution of the Christians, he experienced his Damascus Road conversion followed by a time in the Arabian Desert. After three years he returned to Damascus where the Jews tried to kill him. There he preached in synagogues (Acts 9) and spent some time with Peter in Jerusalem. Then he sailed to Caesarea, on to Tarsus, and there Barnabas found him and brought him back to Antioch (Acts 11). From that point on, the record of Paul's ministry is quite clearly established in the pages of the New Testament.

More than likely during these early years (perhaps in Arabia) he received these marvelous revelations of which he speaks in our chapter (1:12). We can really interpret such direct phraseology in only one way: Paul's authority to proclaim the Gospel and his interpretation of Christian theology depended not upon his rabbinical training but upon direct revelation from God (1 Cor. 11:23).

A. PAUL'S GREETING (*Gal. 1:1-5*). In these few verses, quite typical of epistolary greetings in that time and culture, Paul emphasizes immediately that his apostleship comes from God. He dwells on the connection of the Father and the Son, the Crucifixion, and the magnificence of God's plan in the Gospel.

Examining the Text

1. Read Galatians 1:1-5. What does this greeting tell us about Paul's position of leadership?

He is under God the father through Jesus Christ

2. What are Paul's spiritual qualifications to write this letter? *He is an apostle through Jesus Christ,*

3. Why do you think Paul included a reference to "all the brothers with me" in his greeting?

To recognize and inform about believers with him,

4. What seems to be the focal point of these verses?

Grace and peace through Jesus who gave for us,

Explaining the Text

1. The normal word to begin a Greek letter would have been *rejoice* and the Hebrews would have used *peace*. The use of the word *grace* was distinctly related to Paul.

3. The abrupt designation of the letter "to the churches in Galatia" indicates the seriousness of the content. Paul usually has a word of commendation for the believers to whom he writes, even in the epistles to Corinth.

Explaining the Text

5. The word *rescue* in verse 4 is *exairéo* which means "to pluck out or deliver." The use of the word sets the tone of the epistle—the Gospel emancipates believers from bondage.

Examining the Text

5. See if you can sort out in verses 3-5, what believers have received from the Father and what they have received from the Son.

God raised Jesus from death. Jesus gave himself for our sins to deliver us from evil according to will of g

---

B. PAUL'S PROBLEM (*Gal. 1:6-10*). Paul wastes no time in attacking the error of "Galatianism"—falling back under law after one has been saved by grace. The Christian needs to be tolerant about many things (Romans 14), but the clarity of the Gospel of grace is not one of them. Covering the Gospel of grace with a system of law attacks God's sovereignty and puts salvation back on the shoulders of human beings, expecting them to somehow earn heaven.

Explaining the Text

1. The Greek word for "so quickly" also appears in 1 Timothy 5:22 where the young leader is warned against ordaining anyone without proper evaluation. It emphasizes how soon after trusting Christ the Galatians were rashly accepting the distortions of the Judaizers.

Examining the Text

1. Read Galatians 1:6-10. State in one sentence the problem which gives rise to these verses.

some one is leading them astray — away from Grace toward earning their way to heaven. there is a true gospel

4.

2. How many times does Paul use the term *Gospel* in this passage?

(4)

3. What do you think he means by "a different Gospel"?

a false gospel

Examining the Text

4. About whom does Paul say, "Let him be eternally condemned"?

anyone who preaches a false gospel

5. According to verse 10, what role does motive play in Christian service? *Purpose is to serve God.*

Explaining the Text

4. The word for "eternally condemned" also appears in 1 Corinthians 16:22 where it declares that those who don't love the Lord Jesus are outcasts from the faith. It comes from the Greek word *anathema*.

C. PAUL'S BACKGROUND (*Gal. 1:11-17*). Now Paul turns the argument to his autobiographical credentials. The Gospel of grace came to this man by direct revelation from the Lord. He reviews that process by describing events before his conversion, during his conversion, and after his conversion.

Examining the Text

1. What does Paul tell us about his former life?

Gospel of grace given to him through God not man

2. In what specific ways did Paul change his attitudes and behavior? *Instead of persecuting the Church God prepared him to preach to Gentiles*

3. How does Paul defend his present activities as an apostle?

His information came from God not man,

Explaining the Text

1. Right at the beginning of the section Paul contrasts his authority with the authority of the Judaizers who depended almost exclusively upon the tradition of the elders.

3. Interestingly, throughout Galatians the word *Judaism* appears only in verses 13-14 of this paragraph. Paul apparently thinks it appropriate and perhaps even necessary to affirm his former way of life.

Explaining the Text	Examining the Text
4. The verb *reveal* in verse 16 comes from the root word *apocalypse*, the Greek name for the last book of the New Testament. Paul commonly refers to this personal contact with the Lord (1 Cor. 9:1; 15:8; Phil. 3:12).	4. List the things Paul claims he *did* do and the things he *did not* do. *He went to Arabia and Damascus and to see g. Peter & James*
5. In the New Testament one always goes "up to Jerusalem" (v. 17) since it was on higher ground or in the hill country.	5. Why do you think Paul emphasizes that he didn't consult with any church leaders at the time of his conversion? (vv. 16-17) *he wanted to assure everyone that his up came from God*

D. PAUL'S BEGINNING (*Gal. 1:18-24*). Paul began and ended his ministry well. He wanted his Galatian readers to understand the significance of direct revelation (v. 17) and how the quality of his ministry commended itself to the Jerusalem Christians.

Explaining the Text	Examining the Text
1. The chief city of Cilicia was Tarsus, Paul's home town. Paul's references to geography in Galatians seem to relate specifically to charges brought by the Judaizers, not an attempt to provide a chronology of his life and ministry.	1. Read Galatians 1:18-24. Use a Bible atlas to pinpoint Jerusalem, Arabia, Damascus, Syria, Cilicia, and Judea (vv. 17-22).
2. The word *only* in verse 23 emphasizes Paul's humble and unspectacular beginning as a servant of Christ.	2. Why does going to Jerusalem seem so important to Paul?
	3. What happened when Paul finally did go to Jerusalem? *meet w/ Peter*

Examining the Text	Explaining the Text

Examining the Text

4. What was the end result of Paul's preaching?

they glorified God in me,

5. List two or three things Paul seems to be trying to prove in verses 18-24. *that he grew*
in faith in wilderness
with God separate from C's

6. Count the uses of the first-person pronoun (I) in verses 11-24. Why would Paul refer to himself so frequently? *to establish credibility*

Experiencing the Text

1. How can churches today put into practice the principle of sending out workers in the spirit of verses 1-2?

2. Write down some ways God has rescued you from "the present evil age" (v. 3).

3. In what ways would you advise someone to discern between truth and error?

4. Ask yourself the two questions Paul raises in verse 10.

5. Name some ways your life is different since trusting Jesus as your Saviour.

6. Paul talks about being "extremely zealous for the traditions of my fathers." Do we have any problem with this in the church today? Name some specific examples.

7. Review verse 15. Whom do you know who could say these phrases about himself or herself?

8. In what ways does a Christian establish a reputation in order to create opportunities for ministry?

9. Name some ways your life is presently causing people to praise God (v. 24).

Galatians 2

Welcome to the Church!

Dr. Eugene Williams, Executive Director of American Missionary Fellowship, tells an interesting story about a football game in Spartan Stadium located on the East Lansing campus of Michigan State University. An irate fan, disappointed with the lackluster play by both teams on the field, kept screaming at then coach Duffy Daugherty to call a pass play from quarterback Earl Morrill to end Gene Washington. When the play was finally called, the team gained 29 yards. The excited fan, sitting just two rows behind Dr. Williams, shouted in conclusion, "OK, Duffy, from here you're on your own."

That interesting anecdote applies in two ways to the Book of Galatians. First of all, after emphasizing the uniqueness and dramatic personalization of his own conversion, Paul now wants the Galatians to understand that he was not independent of other believers and church leaders. Maverick that he may have seemed, he was not on his own.

Secondly, the story applies tersely to the general theme of Galatians in which Paul repeatedly emphasizes to these believers that after trusting Christ for salvation through grace by faith, they are not on their own to continue in faith nor to live the Christian life. Sanctification and service, like salvation, come as gifts of God's grace.

In this chapter, Paul continues to defend his apostolic authority and the purity of his Gospel. Now, however, he emphasizes content rather than source and, as suggested above, his interrelationship with other leaders in the early church. One of the central themes of the New Testament is the unity of the body, and Paul understood clearly that any rupture between his work with the Gentiles and the ongoing leadership of Jewish Christians in Palestine would be harmful to both those aspects of the ministry.

This biblical lesson recognizes human as well as divine accountability. It's one thing for a pastor or Christian leader to emphasize that he has been called by God. The Bible has strong documentation for that kind of testimony. But that call must also be authenticated and affirmed by others who have placed themselves under the truth and the control of the Holy Spirit. Ordination and credentialing represent that kind of affirmation in the modern-day church.

Our chapter begins in chronology and geography but culminates in poignant theology. The arguments of where Paul was at what time and with whom seem to pale by the time we read his dramatic testimony in verse 20.

A. RESPONDING IN FAITH (*Gal. 2:1-5*). Paul never wanted the church to divide into Jewish and Gentile branches. Yet he faced and fought that tension throughout his adult life. Here we learn he was willing to invest energy and time to go again to Jerusalem in order to take care of some of these matters.

Explaining the Text

1. This visit to Jerusalem is not a reference to the Jerusalem Council (Acts 15) but rather the delivering of a famine offering (Acts 11:30).

3. The *New English Bible* refers to false brothers as "sham Christians."

6. The word *infiltrate* in verse 4 is used only here and in Romans 5:20. These theological spies wanted to catch Paul abusing his freedom in Christ.

Examining the Text

1. Read Galatians 2:1-5. When Paul went to Jerusalem he was accompanied by Barnabas and Titus. From what you know about the Book of Acts, why would the presence of these two men be important on this visit?

2. For what reason did Paul go to Jerusalem?

3. What exactly did the "false brothers" teach?

4. How did Paul advise the Galatians to respond?

5. How is Paul using "freedom" in this passage?

6. What resulted from Paul's refusal to give in to the false brothers?

Examining the Text	Explaining the Text
7. What brought about the discussion of Titus' circumcision?	
8. What do you think Paul means by "the truth of the Gospel"?	

B. DISAGREEMENTS IN THE FAITH (*Gal. 2:6-10*). The outcome of the visit demonstrated that Paul's ministry with Gentiles and Peter's ministry with Jews were both important. The leaders of the Gentile church at Antioch received "the right hand of fellowship" when the "pillars" at Jerusalem saw the demonstration of God's grace in their work.

Examining the Text	Explaining the Text
1. Read Galatians 2:6-10. What does Paul mean by the phrase "external appearance"? (v. 6)	
2. Why was the opinion of Peter, James, and John so important?	2. Paul's repeated use of an interesting phrase ("seem to be leaders," v. 2; "seem to be important," v. 6; "reputed to be pillars," v. 9) may carry some sardonic and critical tone toward the leaders at Jerusalem.
3. How was Paul encouraged by these three men?	3. The James referred to in this paragraph is the Lord's brother, not John's brother. The familiar "Peter, James, and John" of the Gospels has a new member since the death of John's brother at the hand of Herod (Acts 12).

Explaining the Text	*Examining the Text*
	4. Can you think of another expression for "the right hand of fellowship"?
	5. What was the one requirement the Jerusalem leaders asked of Paul?
	6. From what you know about the two men, why would God choose Peter to preach to the Jews and Paul to the Gentiles?
7. In Paul's mind, the collection from the Gentile churches was a big demonstration of their commitment. He refers to it in Romans 15:26; 1 Corinthians 16:3-4; 2 Corinthians 8–9.	7. What was Paul's attitude toward giving to the poor?

C. JUSTIFIED BY FAITH (*Gal. 2:11-16*). Paul has established his unity with the Jerusalem leaders. Now he wants to demonstrate that the purity of the Gospel is more important even than relationships with other people. Apparently Peter was led to detach himself from Gentile believers and eat only with Jews, a behavior in which he influenced others. Paul reports to the Galatian churches that he confronted Peter publicly, since the issue was not some minor controversy but the implementation of justification by faith.

Explaining the Text	*Examining the Text*
1. The "certain men" of verse 12 are probably to be connected with the "false brothers" of verse 4. The word *hypocrisy*, appearing twice in verse 13, means "playacting," used in classical Greek to describe actors on a stage carrying out roles which did not spring from inner convictions.	1. Read Galatians 2:11-16. After carefully reading verses 11-13, write one sentence about each man mentioned telling what he did and, if possible, why he did it.

Examining the Text	*Explaining the Text*
2. Why didn't Paul confront Peter privately? (v. 14)	
3. What two ways were being taught about how to be justified in God's sight?	
4. In your own words, state the basis of the argument between Paul and Peter.	4. The threefold repetition of the phrase "observing the law" (vv. 15-16) may seem awkward, though we must remember Paul did not have our common word *legalism* to describe the behavior he was attacking.
5. What reasons do you think Peter might have had for acting the way he did? In your opinion did Paul handle the situation correctly?	5. By not fully accepting Gentile believers, Peter pressured them to conform to the standards of the law (circumcision, washings, etc.) in order to gain his approval.

D. LIVING BY FAITH (*Gal. 2:17-21*). Relating the incident with Peter brings Paul back again to the central theme of justification by faith. Now Paul has begun to develop the central message of this letter, and we find in these few verses a capsule of what he expands throughout the rest of the epistle.

Examining the Text	*Explaining the Text*
1. Read Galatians 2:17-21. According to Paul, how does a person begin to realize his or her own sinfulness?	1. The verb form of the word *justification* appears three times in verse 16 and once in verse 17; the noun appears in verse 21.

Explaining the Text

Examining the Text

2. Notice Paul's argument. If Peter goes back to the Law, then he was wrong to leave the Law the first time. His behavior denied the Cornelius experience and his wonderful testimony in Acts 11:4-17.

2. In what ways does God use the Law to bring people to Christ?

3. How many times do the words *live* and *life* appear in verses 19-20?

4. Which of these references refer to physical life and which to spiritual life?

5. Galatians 2:20 emphasizes that our spiritual hope rests on a personal relationship with Christ plus nothing. The power for "living by faith" then comes from the indwelling Saviour, not our own courage or perseverance.

5. In what way is "living faith" made available to us?

Experiencing the Text

1. Think of some ways Christians might abuse their freedom in Christ (v. 4).

2. What are some common areas of disagreement among Christians in this area of freedom?

3. How do we sometimes judge people on "external appearance"?

4. What are you and your church currently doing for the poor? (v.10)

5. When is it right to oppose another Christian?

6. Dealing with Christians you think are wrong, how can you balance Matthew 18:15 and 1 Timothy 5:20?

7. How do some Christians practice discrimination today?

8. Name some areas of your life that have been "crucified with Christ."

9. In what ways have you experienced living by faith in Christ?

10. What difference would it have made to you if Jesus Christ had not died on the cross?

11. Contrast ways of gaining righteousness through the Law with gaining righteousness through God's grace (v.21).

Galatians 3:1-14

Promise of Faith

According to reports from the Aetna Insurance Company, a widow collected $10,000 on a double indemnity insurance policy even though her husband never signed the policy nor paid any premiums on it. Medicus L. Robertson, 32, had been considering a policy. Kenneth K. Specht, an insurance agent, called on him at the TV store where he worked. Mr. Robertson decided to buy a $5,000 policy with double indemnity in the event of accidental death. Mr. Specht filled out a binder, an agreement that would give Mr. Robertson insurance coverage pending a more formal application. At that moment an angry customer walked in and shot Mr. Robertson, killing him immediately. The insurance company paid the $10,000 because the man had verbally agreed to buy the policy. They did, however, deduct the $10.50 premium Mr. Robertson was never able to pay (Kirban Associates, Huntingdon Valley, Pa.).

Promises have deteriorated in our society, a culture which cares little for covenants, and in which a person who keeps his or her word is a rarity. The Bible is full of promises and full of admonitions to keep one's promises. Such behavior, we are told, is modeled after God Himself.

The writer of Hebrews encourages believers by saying, "Let us hold unswervingly to the hope we profess, for He who promised is faithful" (Heb. 10:23). In our passage for this study, the young Christians in the Galatian churches are called to trust in the promises of God, not in their own abilities or behavior. As noted earlier, the problem of the Galatians centered in an unwarranted, unbiblical dependence upon oneself for continuation in the Christian life. These young Christians were engaged in foolish, unreasonable conclusions. After enjoying salvation by grace and freedom from religious rules and rituals, they seemed willing to turn again to the bondage of the Law, persuaded by the slick arguments of the Judaizers. To counter their foolishness the apostle dips into the Old Testament to show that God's plan is centered in promises of faith.

A. THE PROMISE OF THE SPIRIT (*Gal. 3:1-5*). Up to this point Paul has centered his argument in his own experience and calling by God. That argument forces a renewed focus on the Gospel, more particularly on the doctrine of justification by faith. Having shown how this biblical idea worked in his own life, he now aims the doctrine at the Galatians themselves, reviewing their experience with faith and the Holy Spirit.

Examining the Text	*Explaining the Text*
1. Read Galatians 3:1-5. What is Paul's primary concern about the Galatians?	1. The word *portrayed* in verse 1 (*phrographien*) is a word Paul sometimes uses for preaching. It literally means "to post a notice" as on a bulletin board or public sign.
2. How many questions does Paul ask in this paragraph? How many of them can you answer?	
3. Why does Paul seem so stern in the early verses of this chapter?	
4. What were the Galatians doing that Paul disapproved of?	4. "Human effort" in verse 3 is the common Greek word for *flesh* and refers to human nature and its unregenerate weakness apart from faith and the power of God.
5. What did Paul want them to do?	
6. According to these verses, how does a Christian receive the Holy Spirit?	
7. In what way do you think the Galatians may have suffered? (v. 4)	

Explaining the Text	Examining the Text
	8. Do you feel Paul really thought that suffering was for nothing? (v. 4)
9. Notice the first word of verse 5. God's work continues among the Galatians; both verbs describing God's activity are present participles, not just something the Galatians had seen at one time.	9. Find the question Paul asks twice. Why would he emphasize this question?

B. THE PROMISE OF NATIONAL BLESSING (*Gal. 3:6-9*). Bible scholars suggest that Paul raises the Abraham argument for two main reasons. First of all, he wants to demonstrate that the Gospel finds foundation in the history of the Jewish nation, not just in the experience of the New Testament church. Secondly, the Judaizers most likely emphasized their "sons of Abraham through circumcision" argument, probably advancing their false premises from Genesis 12–17.

Explaining the Text	Examining the Text
1. Note that it is the *object* of faith, not the *quality* of faith, that brings the gift of righteousness (v. 6).	1. Read Galatians 3:6-9. In what way was Abraham an example to all people?
2. Paul's general point in the passage is that those who have faith, whether Jews or Gentiles, can be as blessed as Abraham was. The prime characteristic of that blessing is justification.	2. How can Jews and Gentiles alike become children of Abraham?
	3. Look up and review the Old Testament quotations from Genesis 12:3; 15:6; 18:18; 22:18.

Examining the Text	Explaining the Text
4. Why would Paul have chosen these particular quotations out of all the passages he might have used?	
5. Recognizing that "faith" and "believe" come from the same Greek root, count the number of times that idea appears in these four verses.	
6. How was Abraham's faith different from ours?	6. As you might expect, the word for "credited" (v. 6) is a business term rendered in classical Greek in various but similar ways—accounted, placed on deposit, reckoned, etc.
7. Do you find "the Gospel" in this passage? If not, what do you think is missing and why?	

C. THE PROMISE OF REDEMPTION (*Gal. 3:10-14*). On the positive side, Paul has emphasized that people can be saved only by faith. Now he stresses the negative: no one has ever been saved by the Law. Indeed, says Paul, the Law itself teaches that we must be justified by faith and that it is impossible to mix a dependence on the Law with the Gospel of justification by faith.

Examining the Text	Explaining the Text
1. Read Galatians 3:10-14. In one short sentence write Paul's central idea in this paragraph.	1. The curse of the Law is the curse of death (vv. 13-14). Jesus became a curse for us, taking our sins and dying in our place on the cross.
2. What do you think he has in mind when he uses the phrase "book of the Law"?	

Explaining the Text

3. The "us" of verse 13 refers to both Jews and Gentiles, since both received redemption through Christ alone.

4. To "redeem" (v. 14) means to purchase out of slavery for a price.

5. *Righteousness*, as used both in Habakkuk 2:4 and in this paragraph, refers to those who stand in a right relationship to God.

Examining the Text

3. How many times in this paragraph are the words *curse* or *cursed* used?

4. What was the "blessing given to Abraham" that also came to the Gentiles?

5. Review Romans 1:16-17 to see another context in which Paul uses Habakkuk 2:4.

Experiencing the Text

1. How do people today try to gain favor with God through works rather than through faith?

2. According to verse 1, what is one of the first things we need to know about Jesus Christ?

3. By what means do we receive Christ and then continue on in the Christian life?

4. Paul refers to Abraham as a "man of faith." Name some "persons of faith" who have touched your life.

5. In one brief statement explain how you are a child of Abraham.

6. How does your life and family bring blessing to others?

7. Reread verses 1-14 again, writing down every blessing a Christian enjoys because Christ died on the cross.

8. Name some ways Christians today can be "bewitched" by false doctrine.

Galatians 3:15–4:7

From Sinai to Sonship

In his book *Who Switched the Price Tags?* (Word Books), Tony Campolo tells the story of a young graduate of West Point Academy who was sent to Vietnam to lead a group of new recruits into battle. He did his job well, trying his best to keep his men from ambush and death. However, one night he and his men were overtaken by a battalion of Vietcong. He was able to get all but one of his men to safety. The one soldier who had been left behind had been severely wounded, and from their trenches the young lieutenant and his men could hear their wounded comrade moaning and crying for help. They all knew that venturing out into the vicious crossfire of the enemy would mean almost certain death, but the groanings of the wounded soldier continued on through the night.

Eventually the endurance of the young lieutenant came to an end, and he crawled out of his place of safety toward the cries of the dying man. He reached him safely and was able to drag him back. But just as he pushed the wounded man into the safety of the trench he himself caught a bullet in the back and was killed instantly.

Several months later the rescued man returned to the United States, and when the parents of the dead hero heard that he was in their vicinity, they planned to have him come to dinner. They wanted to know this young man whose life was spared at such a great cost to them.

On the night of the dinner party, their guest arrived drunk. He was loud and boisterous. He told off-color jokes and showed no concern for his suffering hosts. The parents of the dead hero did the best they could to make it a worthwhile evening, but their efforts went unrewarded.

At the end of that torturous visit, the obscene guest left. As her husband closed the door, the mother collapsed in tears and cried, "To think that our precious son had to die for somebody like that."

One of the central themes of Galatians is the substitutionary death of Jesus for us. Toward the end of Galatians 3, Paul reminds us that "the whole world is a prisoner of sin," released only because of the death of Jesus Christ. Christ's death took place because of a promise that was never broken, an agreement made with Abraham 430 years before Moses received the Law. Later, because of human sin, God gave the Law on a temporary basis until the promise to Abraham could be fulfilled.

During that time, writes Paul, the Law served as a teacher to point up sin in the human race. It pointed its pedagogical finger at Christ and the Cross. Now that faith has come, we've graduated from school and have put on the freedom and equality found only in Christ.

A. SEED OF ABRAHAM (*Gal. 3:15-18*). Even if Paul's legalistic opponents were willing to grant that Abraham was saved by faith in God's promise, they would probably have argued that the giving of the Law at a later time changed the rules, pushing aside the covenant and instituting law-keeping in its place. Paul sees this argument coming and preempts it by an appeal to the general understanding of human agreements in that and any culture.

Examining the Text	*Explaining the Text*
1. Read Galatians 3:15-18. In this paragraph Paul uses another "example." What is the main point of his illustration?	
2. How did the people to whom Paul refers perceive a human promise?	
3. Which seems to be more important in our passage, the promise given to Abraham or the Law given to Moses?	3. The 430 years of verse 17 may refer to the renewal of the Abrahamic promise to Jacob (Gen. 46:2-4) or to the period between Abraham and Moses (Exodus 12:40).

Explaining the Text	Examining the Text
4. In verse 16 Paul reminds his readers that God, in His promise to Abraham, made a distinction between Isaac and Ishmael. Therefore, the word *seed*, rather than some similar word like *children* or *descendants*, is appropriate.	4. What's Paul's point about "seed" and "seeds"?
5. The word *gave* in verse 18 is based on the word for "grace," emphasizing again that salvation is a free gift from God.	5. What is the inheritance mentioned in verse 18?

B. PRISONERS OF THE LAW (*Gal. 3:19-25*). But if everything depends on God's promise, why was the Law so dominant in the Old Testament? One might even conclude that the Law, with its curses and its temporary nature, actually stood in opposition to God's plan of salvation. Not true, says Paul; for the one who views the Law correctly, it can point to Christ. Only those who depend upon the Law for their own righteousness become its prisoners.

Explaining the Text	Examining the Text
	1. Read Galatians 3:19-25. State in your own words God's purpose for the Law.
2. The word *transgressions* in verse 19 is *parabasis* which refers to the act of a person stepping beyond some fixed boundary. When used for human conduct it can indicate a violation of the rights of others.	2. What do you think Paul means by the statement, "The Law was put into effect through angels by a mediator"? (v. 19)

Examining the Text	Explaining the Text
3. Contrast a life under the Law with a life of faith.	
4. Who is the mediator of verses 19-20? (See 1 Tim. 2:5; Heb. 8:6; 9:15.)	4. Three times the New Testament refers to the involvement of angels in the giving of the Law (Acts 7:53; Gal. 3:19; Heb. 2:2).
5. What does Paul mean when he says "we are no longer under the supervision of the Law"? (v. 25)	5. The phrase "put in charge" in verse 24 is the familiar word *schoolmaster*, designating a slave employed by Greek or Roman families to supervise the behavior of a boy from age 6–16. He was a guardian of morals, not a teacher of academic subjects.
6. In what way can it be said that "the whole world is a prisoner of sin"? (v. 22)	6. The word *Scripture* (v. 22), used in the singular, refers to a particular passage. Here Paul may be thinking of Psalm 143:2 or Deuteronomy 27:26.

C. HEIRS OF THE PROMISE (*Gal. 3:26-29*). Now that faith has come, what difference does it make whether people are Jews or Greeks? Slaves or free? Men or women? None, with respect to their relationship with Christ. The heirs of the promise stand equal before the Cross.

Examining the Text	Explaining the Text
1. Read Galatians 3:26-29. What does it mean to be God's heir?	1. The word *sons* in verse 26 refers to people of full age who have outgrown their need of the guardian.
2. What is the heir's inheritance?	

Explaining the Text	*Examining the Text*
	3. Why do you think Paul used these three specific contrasts to teach that we are one in Christ?
4. Verse 29 emphasizes the unity of the body without regard for race, social status, or sex. Of course, it doesn't remove the distinctions of identity but rather emphasizes how Christians now belong to each other and that unity is far more important than any categories that formerly divided them.	4. According to verse 29, where does a Christian stand in relationship to the promises of God to Israel?
5. Christians are the spiritual seed of Abraham because we are united to him by faith in Christ, his physical descendant; we are heirs to the blessing, though not to the land and other physical dimensions of the promise (v. 29).	5. List five statements in this passage which describe our relationship in Christ.

D. SONS OF GOD (*Gal. 4:1-7*). Sons and heirs grow up. When they do, they are free from constraints of the home. In the same way, believers remained in childlike bondage to the world until God sent Jesus to adopt them as full-grown sons.

Explaining the Text	*Examining the Text*
1. In the eyes of Roman law, the status of a minor child was no different from that of a slave. Paul is attempting to emphasize the standing of people before and after the Gospel frees them from the world.	1. Read Galatians 4:1-7. To what does Paul compare our heirship?

Examining the Text	Explaining the Text
2. To whom does Paul refer when he says "when we were children, we were in slavery" in verse 3?	2. The "basic principles of the world" (v. 3) probably refers to religious ritual imposed upon neophytes, either Jews under the Law or Gentiles trapped in heathen religions.
3. Why do you think it was necessary for Jesus to be "born of a woman" and "born unto the Law"? (v. 4)	
4. What are the full rights of sons and daughters of God?	
5. According to verse 6, what is the dwelling place and ministry of the Holy Spirit?	5. Notice the Trinitarian reference in verse 6—God, Spirit, and Son—all playing separate roles in salvation.
6. Find and list everything this paragraph tells us about Jesus Christ.	6. "Abba" in verse 6 is the term Jesus regularly used for the Father in prayer.

Experiencing the Text

1. In what ways have you seen God keep His promises to you?

2. Evaluate yourself on how well people can expect you to keep your promises and commitments.

3. In what specific ways does the Law of God affect your life?

4. In what specific ways does the grace of God affect your life?

5. How well is your church currently practicing Galatians 3:28? What areas need improvement?

6. These verses use several different terms to describe Christians. Locate each one and see if you think these terms adequately define believers today.

7. How does your understanding of verses 26-28 affect your attitude toward Christ?

8. If we are Abraham's seed (v. 29) how does that make us like Abraham?

9. Name some rights and privileges of being "sons."

10. We can become children of God through faith in Christ and not by keeping the Law—write a prayer of thanksgiving to God for this wonderful truth.

Galatians 4:8-31

Escape from Slavery

Some 30 countries of the world still practice some form of slavery and, in most of those countries, that institution seems likely to continue for some time. In the study before us, Paul likens the bondage that comes from "observing special days and months and seasons and years" to the institution of slavery, well known in the Roman world.

But his metaphor reminds us that slavery is much more complex than the odious indenture of one human being to another. Someone has suggested:

It isn't always others who enslave us. Sometimes we let circumstances enslave us; sometimes we let routines enslave us; sometimes we let things enslave us; sometimes, with weak wills, we enslave ourselves. Sometimes we partake of detrimental things that we think will soothe our nerves, minds, or imaginations—things we think will help us to escape from reality. But no man is free if he is running away from reality. And no man is free if he is running away from himself (*Quotable Quotes*, Victor).

Paul could not understand how the Galatians could turn back to the bondage of paganism, particularly marked by religious ritual of one kind or another. At one time they had welcomed Paul and proclaimed great blessing from his ministry. Can't they see that the Judaizers have impure motives? Don't they understand that falling back into legalism represents regress rather than progress? Can't they see how much Paul wants Christ to be formed in them?

Then the apostle plunges into a fascinating true story which he wants interpreted as an allegory—Ishmael was the son of the Law and Isaac the son of promise. This continuing contrast of freedom and slavery runs throughout the passage.

Through Paul's pen, God couches spiritual truth in historical events. In a moment of tenderness only rarely found in this epistle, Paul pleads with his readers to recognize the contrasts between freedom and slavery. The earthly Jerusalem represented for Paul a position of bondage from which he wants all believers to be released in order that they may be the true children of Abraham.

In his book *God Tells the Man Who Cares*, A.W. Tozer reminds us that "freedom is liberty within bounds: liberty to obey holy laws, liberty to keep the commandments of Christ, to serve mankind, to develop to the full all the latent possibilities within our redeemed natures. . . . True Christian liberty never sets us free to indulge our lusts or to follow our fallen impulses. . . . Freedom is priceless. Where it is present almost any kind of life is enjoyable. When it is absent life can never be enjoyed; it can only be endured."

A. THE SLAVERY OF RITUAL (*Gal. 4:8-11*). Paul's argument now changes to appeal. He reminds the Galatians that they were once slaves in paganism and expresses disbelief that they could consider a return to that condition.

Explaining the Text	*Examining the Text*
	1. Read Galatians 4:8-11. Count how many times Paul uses the words *know* and *known* in this section.
	2. What does he want to emphasize by the use of these words?
3. In other places Paul refers to the gods of this world as "demons" (1 Cor. 8:5-6; 10:19-20; Col. 2:15).	3. Who is Paul talking about when he says "those who by nature are not gods"? (v. 8)
4. Though the highest form of pagan ritual was inferior to the Mosaic Law, they are both referred to here as *stoicheia*, elementary systems of training.	4. What are the "weak and miserable principles"? (v. 9)

Examining the Text	Explaining the Text
5. Why does Paul mention the issue of observing special times?	5. The word *observing* in verse 10 denotes scrupulous and intense care lest any of the prescribed ritual be overlooked. The idea encompasses a cultic allegiance to form.
6. What did Paul fear regarding the behavior of the Galatians?	

B. THE SLAVERY OF ZEAL (*Gal. 4:12-20*). In this section Paul's pastoral heart breaks through his theological case. He refers to his readers as "brothers" and "my dear children," the latter phrase appearing only here in Paul's writings.

Examining the Text	Explaining the Text
1. Read Galatians 4:12-20. How would you describe Paul's emotional state during the writing of this section?	1. The *New English Bible* renders the first part of verse 12, "Put yourselves in my place, my brothers, I beg you, for I have put myself in yours."
2. What primary concern does he express to the Galatians?	
3. In what two ways did the Galatians first welcome Paul?	
4. How did they respond to his illness?	4. We have no idea what Paul's illness was, though the most common guess is some form of eye disease, a conclusion generally connected with verses 15 and 6:1.

Explaining the Text	*Examining the Text*
	5. To whom does Paul refer when he says, "Those people are zealous to win you over"? (v. 17)
6. The word for "formed" (v. 19) describes the act of giving outward expression to one's inner nature. The Greek word is *morphoó* from which we get our biological term "metamorphosis."	6. When did Paul want the Galatians to be zealous and how did he want them to use this zeal? (v. 18)

C. THE SLAVERY OF THE OLD COVENANT (*Gal. 4:21-27*). Meanwhile, Paul redirects the thinking of his readers back to Abraham and his family. The story illustrates and reviews his argument, namely, the contrast between the principle of Law and the principle of faith, between bondage and freedom, between Law and spirit. The allegory leads us from the doctrinal portion of the epistle and Paul's pastoral appeal to the ethical section which begins in Galatians 5.

Explaining the Text	*Examining the Text*
1. Paul's treatment of this passage is precisely the reverse of what it would have been during his days in the Sanhedrin. Pharisees would see the Jews (the people of the Law) as the descendants of Sarah, but Paul assigns them to Hagar.	1. Read Galatians 4:21-27. Review the story of Sarah and Hagar in Genesis 21:1-20.
	2. Why was Isaac so special in the Old Testament record?
3. Paul is well within a common rabbinical style in using an example well-known to most of his	3. Identify what figurative pictures the readers should see in these two women.

Examining the Text	*Explaining the Text*
	readers in order to explain a truth which they have apparently forgotten. In verse 23, Paul points out that Ishmael's birth was not at all unusual, but Isaac was born because of a promise, implying the miraculous intervention of God.
4. How do you understand the phrase "Hagar stands for Mount Sinai in Arabia and corresponds to the present city of Jerusalem"?	4. Hagar represents bondage because she was a bondslave, and all those in bondage are, therefore, her descendants. She corresponds to the Jerusalem of the first century in the sense that the whole legal system of Judaism centered there.
5. Paul speaks of being free—free from what? (v. 26)	
6. How does the quotation from Isaiah 54:1 support Paul's teaching?	
7. What application does Paul make of the Hagar and Sarah record to the situation in Galatia?	
8. What are the Galatians commanded to do as a result of this teaching?	

D. THE SLAVERY OF THE ORDINARY WAY (*Gal. 4:28-31*). While applying the allegory to the Galatians and placing this epistle in the New Testament, God intends the allegory to apply to all believers. This final paragraph identifies the supernatural basis of life in Christ and the necessity to cast out the legalistic false teachers.

Explaining the Text

Examining the Text

1. Read Galatians 4:28-31. In this part of the analogy, how are Christians like Isaac?

2. Who was the "son born in the ordinary way"? To which people at Galatia does Paul apply this historic figure?

3. Note that persecution of Christians will not always come from pagans but, perhaps even more commonly, from nominally religious "half brothers."

3. How was Isaac persecuted by Ishmael?

4. The family sibling rivalry described in this chapter continues to the present hour in Arab-Israeli tensions.

4. In what way were the "Isaacs" in Galatia being persecuted by the "Ishmaels"?

5. The verse of Scripture which the Jews interpreted to mean God's rejection of the Gentiles (Gen. 21:10) is used by Paul to argue for the exclusion of unbelieving Jews.

5. Why can't the slave woman and her son share in the inheritance? (v. 30)

Experiencing the Text

1. What is the difference between knowing God and being known by God? (v. 9)

2. In light of a passage like this, how can we justify our observance of special religious holidays?

3. Think of the times when you have felt the same frustrations Paul expresses in verse 11. Write some ways God helped you deal with them.

4. What can we learn from this chapter, particularly verses 12-16, which will help us minister to people suffering from some illness?

5. In what ways can modern-day Christians be zealous for the Lord?

6. Name some people or organizations who seem to be zealous for the wrong things.

7. How do people live when they fully understand they are free from the Law?

8. What kinds of things do you find motivate obedience to Scripture in your life?

9. Review the last paragraph of the chapter and write a statement telling what it means to you to be a child of promise.

10. Apply Paul's question at the beginning of verse 15 to yourself (if appropriate). What has happened to all of *your* joy?

Galatians 5:1-12

Free at Last

During the funeral of Sir Winston Churchill, a bugler stationed behind the dome of St. Paul's Cathedral in London sounded taps while everyone waited in hushed silence. The melody marked the end of Churchill's long and distinguished life.

But no sooner had the notes of taps died away in that great cathedral than the bugle sounded again, this time to play reveille, the call by which the military world begins a new day. Churchill wished to give testimony to the truth that death only provides a gateway into God's presence.

In the sense of release from pain and suffering, death, that last great enemy of life, offers freedom. Paul, whose illness has been discussed with emphasis in this letter, looked forward to being with Christ and certainly viewed it as a time of freedom.

Civil rights leader Martin Luther King, Jr., whose "I Have a Dream" speech was delivered in Washington, D.C. on August 28, 1963 before more than 200,000 persons who had marched from the Washington Monument to the Lincoln Memorial, lies buried in the Southview Cemetery in Atlanta. The following words, taken from a spiritual, are carved on his tombstone. "Free at last, free at last, thank God Almighty, I'm free at last."

But the freedom of our passage in this study is not the freedom that comes by release from the pain of this life. Paul has been arguing about the bondage of the Law and freedom in Christ for several paragraphs. Indeed, the first verse of Galatians 5 summarizes chapter 4 and introduces Christ as the great liberator who has set believers free from bondage. Of this passage James M. Boice writes,

> Paul has already reached two important goals in his appeal to the Galatians. He has defended his apostleship, including a defense of his right to preach the gospel with or without the support of other human authorities (1:11–2:21), and he defends the gospel itself, showing it is by grace alone entirely apart from human works that

the Christian is freed from the curse of the law and brought into a right relationship with God (3:1–4:31). But there is one more point to be made before Paul concludes his letter: that the liberty into which believers are called is not a liberty that leads to license, as his opponents would charge, but rather a liberty that leads to mature responsibility and holiness before God through the power of the indwelling Holy Spirit. This theme dominates the last two chapters of the Epistle (*Expositor's Bible Commentary*, vol. 10, Zondervan).

A. FREEDOM FROM DEBT (*Gal. 5:1-3*). Circumcision continues as Exhibit A of a legalistic lifestyle. The act itself presented no problem; the danger to the Galatians lay in Judaistic insistence that circumcision was necessary for salvation. Remember too, writes Paul, anybody who puts himself under even one facet of the Law stands debtor to the entire code.

Explaining the Text	*Examining the Text*
1. This is one place where the chapter divisions are not helpful. We can see the strong connection between the argument of chapter 4, particularly verse 31, and the first verse of chapter 5.	1. Read Galatians 5:1-3. Against what were the Galatians to stand firm? (v. 1)
	2. Describe in other words the "yoke of slavery" (v. 1).
3. The word *if* in verse 2 reminds us that the Galatians had not yet stooped to circumcision for salvation, but they were thinking seriously about it.	3. Why does Paul speak out so strongly against circumcision? (v. 2)
4. Circumcision keeps coming up because without it no amount of conformity to the Law would matter in the eyes of a strict Jew.	4. Why would being circumcised obligate a person to the whole Law? (v. 3)

Examining the Text	Explaining the Text
Examining the Text 5. What does Paul mean by the threat, "Christ will be of no value to you at all"?	*Explaining the Text*

B. FREEDOM FROM FEAR (*Gal. 5:4-6*). Paul now turns to serious "threats" to alert the Galatians to the danger of their position. He tells them if they return to circumcision and law-keeping they have abandoned the "grace system" for a "work system," which he has already shown to be totally bankrupt with regard to salvation. For those in Christ Jesus, however, neither circumcision nor the lack of it makes any difference—"the only thing that counts is faith expressing itself through love."

Examining the Text	*Explaining the Text*
1. Read Galatians 5:4-6. How do you understand the phrase "fallen away from grace"? (v. 4)	1. Remember the Galatians were already saved but, in their minds, they were trying to add to justification by faith through seeking an additional justification by works (v. 4).
2. What is the "free" way to justification? (v. 5)	2. The phrase "eagerly await" (v. 5) is used seven times in the New Testament about the return of Christ (Rom. 8:19, 23, 25; 1 Cor. 1:7; Gal. 5:5; Phil. 3:20; Heb. 9:28).
3. What is Paul's basic point when he says that neither circumcision nor uncircumcision has value? (v. 6)	
4. What enables us to wait for whatever God has for us? (v. 5)	

Explaining the Text	Examining the Text
5. Note that these verses combine again those three great words of the New Testament—faith, hope, and love (1 Cor. 13; Col. 1, 4–5; 1 Thess. 1:3).	5. Name some ways that faith expresses itself through love (v. 6).

C. FREEDOM FROM HARASSMENT (*Gal. 5:7-12*). Beginning with his favorite metaphor (*running*) Paul expresses his confidence in Christ's keeping power for the Galatians. In harsh language he attacks the legalistic false teachers who have harassed both the Galatians and Paul himself. Since they are still at work, the offense of the Cross still stands with those who preach the Gospel.

Explaining the Text	Examining the Text
	1. Read Galatians 5:7-12. Why does Paul refer to the race in the past tense? (v. 7)
2. The phrase "cut in on you" is a military term usually used to describe setting up an obstacle or breaking up a road.	2. To whom does Paul refer when he asks "who cut in on you?" (v. 7)
	3. Who is "the one who calls you"?
	4. Why is yeast an appropriate analogy for what was happening in Galatia?
	5. On what basis can Paul be so confident about people who seem to be readily following false teaching? (v. 10)

Examining the Text	Explaining the Text
6. What do you think is "the penalty" of verse 10?	
7. Why do the accusation and persecution against Paul not make any sense? (v. 11)	
8. What does Paul mean by "the offense of the Cross"? (v. 11)	8. The word *offense* (v. 11) is *skandalon*, meaning "trap" or "snare." The natural man considers the message of salvation through the Cross a scandal.

Experiencing the Text

1. In what ways can we stand firm in our Christian freedom?

2. How do you see people today trying to be justified by works?

3. How should Christians express their faith through love in the family or in the church?

4. What barriers keep you from running a good race?

5. How do we determine in today's church who teaches the truth and who teaches error?

6. With Paul as our model, how should we respond when accused or criticized falsely?

7. Memorize Galatians 5:6b.

8. Describe some modern dangers in teaching people that they have complete freedom and do not live by the Law.

9. What things do we need to do in order to live a balanced life of salvation through grace and yet obedient godliness?

10. How would you apply the proverb of verse 9 today?

11. What implications does this passage have for church discipline?

Galatians 5:13-26

Living by the Spirit

In his historical novel *Alaska*, James Michener tells the story of a ship-wreck. At 7:30 on Wednesday night, August 22, 1906, the Canadian ship *Montreal Queen* plowed headlong into a submerged ledge near Walrus Rock in the southeast Alaskan inland waterway. The captain's emergency cable to his home office received the following response: "If damage not totally disabling, you are ordered to await arrival of *Ontario Queen* speeding to rescue all passengers." This procedure sought to ward off an involvement in profits that might be gained by other rescue ships taking cargo or passengers off the *Queen.*

But when dawn broke Friday morning, the ship disappeared into the dark waters of the inlet and not a single passenger of the 309 on board survived. To prevent a financial loss of $2,000, everyone aboard the *Montreal Queen*, including the crew, perished.

Michener's account aims to show greed, carelessness for life, lack of leadership by the captain, and a terrible deficiency in value choice. In the second half of Galatians 5, Paul moves from a discussion of salvation by faith to the appropriate selection of Christian values in ethical living. Christians can only live for Christ through the power of the Spirit. Like the captain of the *Montreal Queen*, they must make choices between those things which represent "the acts of the sinful nature" and "the fruit of the Spirit."

Like the first century, the culture surrounding believers today offers no help toward the proper choices. The values of pagan society have always been a reversal of God's standards. The *Gannett Center Journal* has researched an estimate of monies spent on sports gambling between 1976 and 1986.

In 1976 the amount spent on all sports, 20 billion; in 1981, 50 billion for NFL only; in 1984 for all sports, 70 billion. That is 70,000 millions of dollars. In three years you could buy all the church and synagogue property with it. If in the time of the Second Crusade and the days of Abelard, the time when Moscow was first mentioned anywhere, the time of Thomas à Becket and the founding of Paris University and Frederick Barbarossa in the middle of the twelfth century "you" would have started giving "me" a dollar a second, you would by now have caught up with last year's estimated illegal sports gambling (described by Martin Marty in *Context*, February 15, 1988, p. 1).

Such is the value system of the world, but this study affirms that Christ calls us to a different kind of lifestyle. He empowers us to live in spiritual freedom and regularly practice the fruit of the Spirit.

A. SERVE ONE ANOTHER (*Gal. 5:13-15*). Freedom is important, but God does not give it so His children can do anything they want to. Rather, we must respond to freedom by applying it constructively in our relationships with other people.

Explaining the Text

1. The phrase "sinful nature" in verse 13 is crucial to this section, appearing in verses 13, 16, 17, 19, and 24. Also rendered by the English word "flesh," the expression refers to the sinner's capacity for evil apart from the intervention of God in his life.

3. The word for "serve" in verse 13 describes a slave's total commitment of all personal privileges and rights to the authority of his master. Paul obviously uses a play on words, telling the Galatians that if they want to be slaves to something, they should be slaves to one another.

Examining the Text

1. Read Galatians 5:13-15. What should be the specific result of freedom in Christ?

2. Toward what improper ends might some use Christian freedom?

3. Compare these verses with verse 6. How are they alike? How are they different?

Examining the Text	Explaining the Text
4. Review the original context of this "single command" in Leviticus 19.	4. The idea of the Law being summed up in one sentence was common among the rabbis and was affirmed by Jesus (Matt. 22:39; Luke 10:25-28).
5. What happens when people continually fight with each other?	

B. LIVE IN THE SPIRIT (*Gal. 5:16-18*). Rather than placing some legalistic curbs on the flesh, Christ calls us to spiritual freedom. Believers led by the Spirit of God are no longer controlled by the Law.

Examining the Text	Explaining the Text
1. Read Galatians 5:16-18. How does life in the Spirit evidence itself?	
2. What are the signs of a life being lived in the flesh?	2. Though evil desires will accompany the believer throughout his life, he can refuse them if he depends upon the power of the Holy Spirit to do so.
3. How many times does the phrase "sinful nature" appear in just these few verses?	3. The double use of the word *contrary* in verse 17 emphasizes the antagonism between fleshly living and spiritual living.
4. What is the difference between living by the Spirit (v. 16) and being led by the Spirit (v. 18)?	4. In only one other place in his writings does the Apostle Paul refer to being led by the Spirit (Rom. 8:14). Both represent dramatic affirmations of the believer's position in Christ.

Explaining the Text	Examining the Text
	5. On the basis of all we have seen in previous studies, what does Paul mean by the statement "You are not under Law"? (v. 18)

C. REJECT THE SINFUL NATURE (*Gal. 5:19-21*). Paul is now ready to provide two checklists for measuring the conduct of people who claim to be related to God. The first (in these verses) describes those who live by the sinful nature. If one's life is marked by the characteristics of this list, he is either not a believer or not under the control of God's Spirit.

Explaining the Text	Examining the Text
1. These behaviors of the flesh are characteristic of those who have not accepted God's grace. They still operate by law which leads to consistent failure.	1. Read Galatians 5:19-21. Count the number of behaviors which describe the sinful nature.
2. "Witchcraft" is a translation of the Greek word *pharmakeia* from which we get our English word "pharmacy." As in our day, so in the ancient world the worship of satanic powers was often accompanied by the use of drugs.	2. Which ones sin against the body?
3. Remember that the Galatians were believers, so the passage suggests that Christians can also be trapped into this kind of behavior if they do not depend upon the Spirit.	3. Which ones deal more with the mind and spirit?
4. Just in case the Galatians were troubled by any sins Paul did not list, he adds the phrase, "and the like."	4. Which ones sin against other people?

Examining the Text	*Explaining the Text*
5. What is the final end of people who live by the flesh?	

D. PRACTICE THE FRUIT OF THE SPIRIT (*Gal. 5:22-26*). Who needs a law to practice the nine things Paul describes in verses 22-23? No one; law has nothing to do with it. But any ability to demonstrate the fruit of the Spirit comes by grace and therefore provides no tribute to the personal righteousness of the believer. Conceit is preempted by a recognition of grace.

Examining the Text	*Explaining the Text*
1. Read Galatians 5:22-26. How do you think the fruit of the Spirit differs from the gifts of the Spirit described in 1 Corinthians 12 and Romans 12?	1. Some suggest three categories of three fruits each: attitudes toward God, attitudes toward other people, and attitudes toward oneself.
2. Identify which behaviors in this list reflect an attitude toward God.	2. Christian joy differs from worldly happiness in that the latter depends on circumstances whereas the former does not.
3. Which behaviors reflect an attitude or action toward other people?	
4. How does one go about crucifying the sinful nature? (v. 24)	
5. Memorize the nine fruits of the Spirit by memorizing Galatians 5:22-23.	5. The word *peace* occurs 80 times in the New Testament and appears in every book.

Experiencing the Text

1. How do you respond to people who feel that grace allows them to live any way they please?

2. How do you deal with the conflict between the sinful nature and the Holy Spirit in your own life?

3. Name some practical ways you can carry out Paul's admonition to "serve one another in love" (v. 13).

4. Why do you think Paul lists so many sinful acts?

5. If he were writing the list to churches today, how would it be different?

6. In what practical ways does one go about crucifying the sinful nature? (v. 24)

7. How do Christians "keep in step with the Spirit"? (v. 25)

8. Read verses 16-26 again. How many times does Paul mention the Spirit? What does this suggest about the emphasis of the passage?

9. Conceit and envy seem clear, but what does it mean to "provoke each other"? (v. 26)

10. Listed below are the nine fruits of the Spirit. Beside each one write a brief sentence to describe how you want the Holy Spirit to make that fruit evident in your life.

Love

Joy

Peace

Patience

Kindness

Goodness

Faithfulness

Gentleness

Self-control

Galatians 6

Liberty and Responsibility

Karl Wallenda, the famous tightrope walker, put his life on the line every time he walked on the high wire. He was so captivated by his work that he once said, "Being on the tightrope is living. Everything else is waiting."

He never thought about failure, until the last day, when he fell to his death in 1978 while walking a high wire in downtown San Juan. Mrs. Wallenda said later, "All Karl thought about for three straight months was falling. It was the first time he had thought about that, and it seemed to me he put all his energies into not falling rather than walking the tightrope." She said he even supervised the installation of the guywires, something he had never done before. His concern became a self-fulfilling prophecy. As long as he was focused on success, he succeeded. When he focused on falling, he fell. (As told by William H. Spoor in a speech at Dartmouth College, February 13, 1986.)

Paul talks a lot about failure in this letter, notably the potential back-sliding of the Galatians into a legalistic system of salvation. But the letter ends with an emphasis on success. Understanding what the fruit of the Spirit is and how it works, the believer is to deliberately practice the kind of lifestyle characterized by the nine fruits listed at the end of Galatians 5. But that is not done in a vacuum. We share the Christian journey with other pilgrims and in this final chapter Paul offers some guidelines.

The Christian life is determined by the choices we make, and Paul wants the Galatians to reject legalism and choose liberty. But with that liberty comes a responsibility toward the truth, toward spiritual life, and toward other people.

All of this seems so important to the apostle that he writes the conclusion of the letter with his own hand rather than using the assistance of a scribe. He reviews various points of the letter—the offense of the Cross, the hypocrisy of the legalizers, the futility of circumcision—and concludes by calling the Galatians "the Israel of God."

The letter to the Galatians was Martin Luther's lecture subject at Wittenberg University in the fall of 1516. One year later he posted his 95 Theses on the church door and the Protestant Reformation began. Galatians has been called the "Magna Charta" of the church because of its repeated emphasis on spiritual freedom in Christ.

A. BEARING AND SHARING (*Gal. 6:1-6*). What does life look like when characterized by the fruit of the Spirit? Rather than mysticism or spiritual fantasy, Paul gets right down to basics—personal relationships and the use of money.

Examining the Text	*Explaining the Text*
1. Read Galatians 6:1-6. What attitude does Paul encourage among believers?	1. The word for "burden" in verse 2 is *baros* and means load of difficulty. At the end of verse 5 "load" translates *phortion* and means responsibility. Christians handle their own responsibilities but share one another's difficulties.
2. What is the proper procedure when another Christian sins?	
3. How can we carry each other's burdens?	3. The word for "carry" (*bastazo*) appears four times in the epistle (5:10; 6:2, 5, 17).
4. Why would Paul encourage pride? (v. 4)	
5. In what ways can we share with those who are our instructors?	5. The reference to "sharing good things" in verse 6 is probably intended to emphasize financial support for teachers of the Scriptures.

B. SOWING AND REAPING (*Gal. 6:7-10*). Now Paul applies the familiar law of the harvest in a section which some have called "the agriculture of the Spirit." Verses 9-10 contain two dramatic guidelines for effective Christian living, the first more personal and the second related to the corporate life of the body.

Explaining the Text	*Examining the Text*
	1. Read Galatians 6:7-10. Why does the illustration of the harvest seem particularly appropriate for the point that Paul wants to make here?
2. The word for "mock" in verse 7 conveys the idea of physical behavior (such as turning up the nose) which points up the hypocrisy of words.	2. How are people deceived when they believe they can sin and not get caught?
3. It's not hard to picture Paul thinking about himself as he writes verse 9, particularly in light of the problems he has faced in Galatia and Corinth.	3. Why do you think it was necessary for Paul to remind people not to "become weary in doing good"? (v. 9)
4. The Greek text uses the same word translated "time" in verse 9 and "opportunity" in verse 10. The word conveys the idea of the appropriate moment or season to do something.	4. What is the harvest? When will we reap?
	5. What group of people should be the primary recipients of a Christian's good works? (v. 10)

C. UNCIRCUMCISION AND CIRCUMCISION (*Gal. 6:11-15*). As the letter draws to a close, the apostle can't resist one more attack on the legalizers, and particularly the issue of circumcision. If the Galatian believers yield to their teaching, there will be boasting, a behavior Paul reserves for the Cross of the Lord Jesus Christ.

Examining the Text	*Explaining the Text*
1. Read Galatians 6:11-15. Why do you think Paul emphasizes that he writes this section with his own hand?	
2. What is the significance of mentioning "large letters"?	
3. What two things motivate those who push for circumcision? (v. 12)	3. The Greek word rendered "make a good impression" suggests insincerity and hypocrisy.
4. What is the "new creation" of verse 15? (See 2 Cor. 5:17.)	4. The phrase "boast about your flesh" at the end of verse 13 suggests that the legalizers would receive great praise in the eyes of their Jewish friends everywhere if they could force the Galatian Christians to circumcision.
5. What two things happened to Paul because of the Cross?	5. The concept of "world" in verse 14 refers to the entire world system with its human religions, secular values, and dependence upon sinful nature.

D. PEACE AND MERCY (*Gal. 6:16-18*). Paul wants all troublemakers to leave him alone, a happy state which he never achieved. Does any Christian doubt his sincerity or his zeal for the truth? Let him look even at the apostle's body where a sacred "scarship" identifies him with the Christ of the Cross.

Explaining the Text	*Examining the Text*
	1. Read Galatians 6:16-18. How is peace evidenced in a Christian's life?
2. The phrase "Israel of God" must refer to Jewish believers; all 65 other occurrences of the word *Israel* in the New Testament refer to Jews.	2. To what "rule" does Paul refer in verse 16?
3. The word "marks" (*stigma*) comes from a verb meaning to stick or inscribe like a tattoo or a brand on a slave (see Rev. 14:9-11).	3. What do you think he meant by "the marks of Jesus"?
	4. Why would Paul select peace and mercy out of all the possible virtues he might wish for his readers?

Experiencing the Text

1. What is your reaction when you hear about a Christian brother or sister who has fallen into sin? How does your reaction measure up to the guidelines of verses 1-5?

2. How can we determine who is spiritual enough to assist in the restoration of a sinning believer?

3. List some ways your family can help carry each other's burdens.

4. In what ways do you share "all good things" with people who have taught you the Scriptures?

5. Name some seeds we can sow "to please the Spirit."

6. List some of your major life goals. How do they measure up to verse 14?

7. Name some ways Christians do good "to all people" (v. 10).

8. Name some ways Christians do good "to those who belong to the family of believers" (v. 10).

9. How does becoming a new creation in Christ make possible avoiding the attitudes of the world?

10. Memorize Galatians 6:9-10, 14.